Kitnor's Tearooms at Bossington

Tearoom and Pub Walks on Exmoor

Robert Hesketh

Bossiney Books

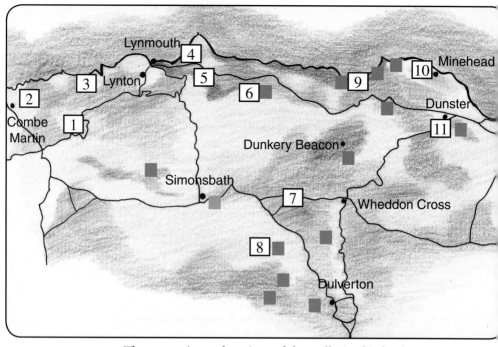

The approximate locations of the walks in this book.
The green squares represent walks in a companion volume,
'Shortish Walks on Exmoor': these are shorter – 6-9 km in length.

All the walks in this book were checked prior to publication, at
which time the instructions were correct. However, changes can
occur in the countryside over which neither the author nor
the publisher has any control. Please let us know
if you encounter any serious problems.

First published 2019 by
Bossiney Books Ltd, 67 West Busk Lane, Otley, LS21 3LY
www.bossineybooks.com

This book contains material originally published in *Exmoor Pub Walks*
and *North Devon Pub Walks* but all the walks were checked in 2018.

© 2019 Robert Hesketh All rights reserved
ISBN 978-1-906474-76-8

Acknowledgements
The maps are by Graham Hallowell
All photographs are by the author www.roberthesketh.co.uk

Printed in Great Britain by R Booth Ltd, Penryn, Cornwall

Introduction

At between 8km and 13.5km (5 and 8 1/2 miles), these 11 walks are long enough to justify some refreshment, either part-way round or at the beginning/end. All of them have at least one pub, and many have tea-rooms or cafés as well. Please be aware that out of season these businesses may be closed, so check in advance. And alas, pubs and cafés sometimes close permanently, though we think it unlikely that any of our choices will.

Some of the walks could be completed in a morning or afternoon. The time you need depends on how fast you walk and how interested you are in what you see – and each walk has several extras, from historic churches to prehistoric monuments.

Exmoor is a walker's paradise, criss-crossed with well signed walks and a great variety of scenery in a relatively small area. High moorland and sea cliffs, rolling hills cut by fast flowing rivers and steep, wooded valleys – the moor is endlessly enjoyable. It also has its own breed of wild pony and is the last stronghold of England's largest mammal, the red deer. The hunting tradition remains central to local life.

Safety (please take seriously)

Walking Exmoor is safe and trouble-free – but be prepared, especially for sudden changes in the weather. Despite a generally mild climate, high winds and fogs are not unknown – not to mention rain! Good walking boots and suitable clothing, including waterproofs, are a must – so are drinking water, a map (Ordnance Survey OL9), compass and a comfortable rucksack. Many, including me, add a walking stick, mobile phone and food to the list.

Ticks are a potential nuisance, especially in hot, humid weather. Wearing long trousers and socks offers some protection against these tiny parasites, which can carry a viral infection, Lyme disease. Remove ticks carefully from your skin as soon as possible.

Access

Unenclosed moorland areas are generally open. Please keep to the paths over enclosed farmland, use (and close) gates as appropriate and keep dogs under control.

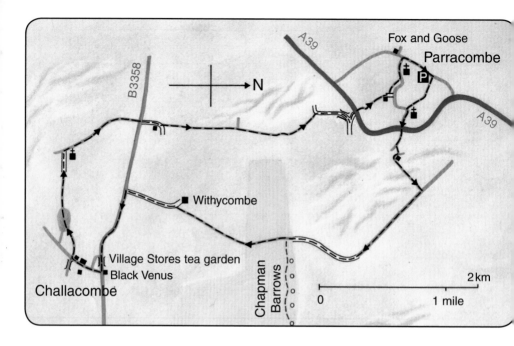

Walk 1   Parracombe and Challacombe

Distance: 13.4 km (8¼ miles) excluding diversion   Time: 4½ hours
Character: Mostly field paths and some open moor, but also 1 km along
a B-road. Some long steady climbs but no really demanding slopes. The
walk connects two attractive Exmoor villages, each with a historic
church and inn. Challacombe's Village Stores serves refreshments
including cream teas, but there is only outside seating.

There are magnificent views on this walk, as well as a group of
prehistoric burial mounds and a view of a Norman motte and bailey
castle. A compass may be useful.

Start from Parracombe's car park, 100 m uphill from Bodley Cross
and just downhill from Heddon Hall. Walk uphill for 150 m and take
the footpath on the right. This emerges by a bridge spanning the old
Lynton & Barnstaple Railway.

Turn left, PUBLIC BRIDLEWAY A39. Follow the bridleway uphill, pass-
ing St Petrock's church (unspoilt Georgian interior). Cross the A39
and take the BRIDLEWAY PARRACOMBE COMMON to a junction 250 m
ahead, and take the left fork (PARRACOMBE COMMON).

Turn right at a T-junction of tracks, PARRACOMBE COMMON. Follow

4

the track past a house and up to another T-junction. Turn right and follow the straight tarmac drive, later a track, for 2 km over Parracombe Common to a gate.

Divert left to see Chapman Barrows, one of Exmoor's most impressive groups of Bronze Age burial mounds. Keep the wall on your left and climb the ladder stile at the top corner. The first of the barrows is on the other side. To see more barrows, you could continue in the same direction to the triangulation point on the summit, which would add 1.6 km (a mile) to the length of the walk.

Retrace your steps to the gate and turn left, WITHECOMBE GATE. Walk south over rough grass (the path may well be indistinct) to a gate in the wall ahead. Follow the bridleway downhill through several more gates. Pass Withycombe Farm and continue down a concrete track to the B3358. Turn left along it for 1.1 km to the Black Venus.

Take the lane opposite the inn and cross the ford 50 m ahead by the footbridge. Walk on past the chapel. Ignore the first footpath on your right. At Rooksfoot, a characteristic Exmoor packhorse bridge, turn right, FOOTPATH CHALLACOMBE. Continue via gates. Bear right (CHALLACOMBE CHURCH) and up through a wood. Cross the fields ahead to the whitewashed church.

Turn right and follow the lane to Yelland Cross. Walk ahead, PUBLIC BRIDLEWAY TWINEWORTHY. Just past the entrance to 'West Whitefield', bear left onto the bridleway as signed, and turn right up

the field. Follow the blue waymarks of the bridleway north through fields, over the rougher grass of Challacombe Common, then down through a sloping field to a metal gate. Now keep the hedge on your left. Reaching a track, turn right at a blue marker.

Follow the track down and over a bridge, then uphill, first curving right then turning sharp left. Cross the A39, FOOTPATH PARRACOMBE. Follow waymarks across the fields to an enclosed lane. Only 40m ahead, turn left through a gate. Turn right and follow the yellow waymarks along the field edge and into an enclosed lane, for Parracombe.

Go through the yard of Sunnyside Farm, then bear left (PUBLIC FOOTPATH PARRACOMBE) across fields and a stream. Turn left to Christ Church, where the churchyard offers a fine view of Holwell, one of hundreds of Norman motte-and-bailey castles built across England after 1066. Follow the lane downhill to a T junction. Turn right uphill, past Bodley Cross to the car park – or divert left to the Fox and Goose.

The Black Venus

The Black Venus is an ancient drovers' inn and may derive its unique name from a breed of sheep, difficult to shear and giving worthless wool. It was formerly the Ring of Bells, as historic photos in the bar show.

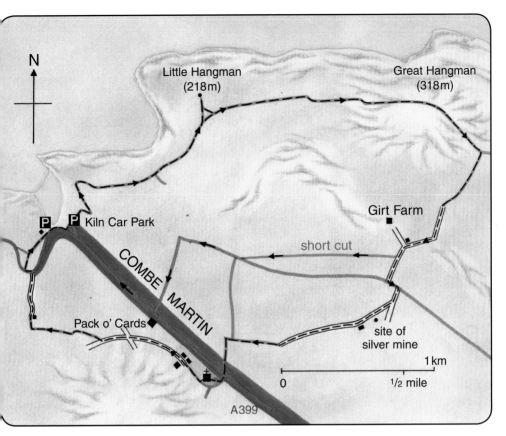

Walk 2   Combe Martin and the Pack o' Cards

Distance: 9.1 km (5³/₄ miles) Time: 3 hours
Character: The climb to Great Hangman – at 318 m the highest point
on the South West Coast Path – is rewarded with spectacular views.
The return includes old silver mines, a medieval church with a superb
carved screen, and a unique inn.

From the Kiln car park at the seaward end of Combe Martin, take the
signed coast path towards the east.

Winding around gardens and up onto the cliffs, the path is clear
and stepped where really steep. Little Hangman (218 m) is reached by
a slight diversion from the main path, but gives wonderful views. The
path to the cairn on the top of Great Hangman is a gentler ascent.

From there, follow the coast path downhill to a fingerpost set in the
corner of a stone wall. Turn right, COUNTY ROAD. Keep the wall on

your left. Continue over a stile and into a farm track.

Bear left at a house onto FOOTPATH COMBE MARTIN. Walk up the concrete track to the next fingerpost. (You could take a short cut by turning right, COMBE MARTIN VIA KNAP DOWN LANE, reducing the walk by 1.4 km.)

For the full route, continue ahead, SILVER MINES. Turn left at the tarred lane and after 50 m turn right down a broad track. When the track divides, bear right. On your left are the ivy-covered remains of the old silver mines (private property). The path descends steeply past Silver Mines Farm, after which it deteriorates.

Continue downhill to the town. Cross HIGH STREET into CHURCH STREET. Turn right up BOWLING GREEN LANE to visit the church. Leave by the lych gate and turn right, PUBLIC FOOTPATH PARK HILLS. This climbs steadily, giving good views of the Hangmen, of Combe Martin's main street, said to be the longest in England, and of the Pack o' Cards.

Fork right from the stony track when a clear level beaten path appears. Ignore the gate on the right but continue ahead, keeping the hedge on your right. Then turn right through a wicket gate with a footpath sign. Follow the enclosed path downhill to a gate, then continue along the driveway to the main road.

Cross the road and turn left along the grass verge for 30 m, then

turn right, PUBLIC FOOTPATH, Keep going downhill, and follow the road out to the Parade, then turn left back down to the Kiln car park.

Whilst there are pubs and cafés near the harbour, you may want to drive 1 km up the High Street to the Pack o' Cards.

The Pack o' Cards

The Pack o' Cards was built in 1690 by George Ley, the squire of Combe Martin. After winning handsomely at cards, he promised 'an everlasting monument to Lady Luck'. The Pack is inspired by a deck of 52 playing cards. It is 52 ft square, has four storeys to represent the four suits, 52 windows and 52 steps in the staircase. There are 13 doors on each floor, and 13 fireplaces.

The four chimneys on the top floor represent the four kings, and the four chimneys below the four queens. The squire's study has 13 panes of glass, whilst the joker window is incomplete.

For over a century the Pack was the Leys' family home. It became an inn during the early nineteenth century: the list of landlords goes back to 1822. This fascinating folly was derelict in 1985. Happily it was restored from 1991, as the inn's museum explains.

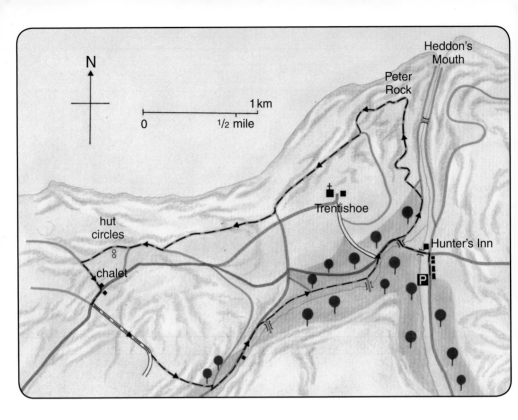

Walk 3   Hunter's Inn and Trentishoe

Distance: 9.7 km (6 miles)
Time: 3 hours
*Character: A steep climb from Heddon's Mouth Cleave is rewarded with
spectacular aerial views of this deep rocky valley and the beach below.
The coast path then has dramatic views of steep cliffs. Vertigo sufferers
might have a problem, and short stretches of scree demand particular
care. The path could also be dangerous in high winds. The return route
via deep woodland provides a remarkable contrast.*

Turn left out of the National Trust car park near Hunter's Inn and
walk down the lane to the inn. Take the COMBE MARTIN road. Turn
right after 300 m, FOOTPATH HEDDON'S MOUTH.

 After 450 m, turn left COAST PATH COMBE MARTIN. The steep ascent
is relieved by zigzags. Take care where there are loose stones (scree).
The path levels out towards Peter Rock, a wonderful viewpoint.

 Follow the Coast Path west along the high cliffs for 3.6 km, ignoring

several turnings left. Start thinking about turning inland when the Coast Path passes through a gap in a stone wall. Immediately beyond this, on the left, there are Bronze Age hut circles, likely to be concealed by bracken in summer.

The sloping roof of a chalet then appears on the left. After another 200 m or so the stony path meets a broad track. Turn sharp left (FOOT-PATH COUNTY ROAD) and follow the track past the chalet to a tarmac lane. Turn right and follow the lane for 150 m. Turn left onto a broad track over Holdstone Down. After 700 m, leave the track, which curves away to the right. Follow the grassy path ahead, downhill and into a wood. Descend quite steeply to a broader path, and turn sharp right along it.

When you reach a tarmac lane, turn left and follow it for 750 m, then bear right, PUBLIC FOOTPATH HUNTERS INN. Continue ahead on this broad woodland path, following a series of HUNTERS INN signs and ignoring side turnings, until you reach a tarmac lane. Turn right and follow it back to Hunter's Inn and the car park – where the National Trust has a shop and ice-cream parlour.

Hunter's Inn, owned by the National Trust
The bar is open all day and provides tea and coffee. Light meals and full three course lunches and dinners are offered, plus cream teas in the afternoons.

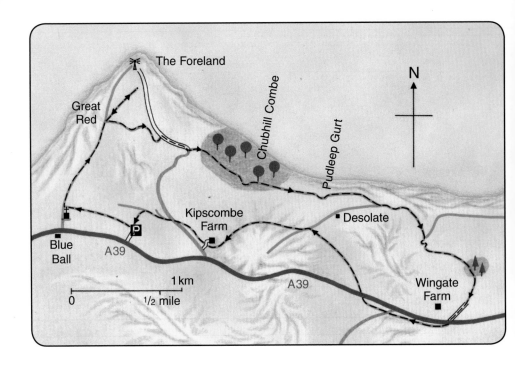

Walk 4   Countisbury

Distance: 11.7 km (7 1/4 miles) including the summit of Foreland
Time: 3 3/4 hours. Can be shortened to 9.2 km (5 3/4 miles) or else
combined with Walk 5 to make an all-day walk.
Character: Towering more than 210 m above the sea, with dramatic
scree slopes, Foreland Point offers magnificent views and is one of
Exmoor's most impressive sights. The walk also includes a fine section
of the coast path, magnificent rhododendrons in May, and a pleasant
inland return. One steep ascent.

Start from the National Trust's Barna Barrow car park (SS 753496).
With your back to the road, turn left and follow the path with the
stone wall on your left. After visiting the church, either take the south
gate to visit the Blue Ball or leave by the north gate and take the COAST
PATH north along the contour of the cliffs. Continue ahead at the next
path junction, PORLOCK.

A deep gash in the cliffs is called Great Red. Turn right on the Coast
Path, or follow the rough path to the crest of the cliffs for the best
views, then retrace your steps to continue along the Coast Path.

Follow the path downhill to a tarred lane. Unless you wish to divert left along the lane to the lighthouse, turn right and follow the lane uphill. At the top of the slope, walk ahead on the Coast Path. The path continues over a stile and on to Glenthorne Cliffs and Chubhill Wood, where gnarled oaks cling bravely to the scree slopes.

Beyond Chubhill Wood, choose either the short cut (COUNTISBURY) reducing the walk by 2.5km (1 1/2 miles), and rejoin the directions where asterisked, or continue along the coastpath for the full route.

Turn right off the coastpath at the next fingerpost, by a brook COUNTY GATE VIA OLD BARROW. Follow the yellow waymarks up a steep slope. Continue across a field and through a conifer plantation. Bear right at the next fingerpost, WHITE POST COUNTISBURY. The path emerges onto the main road. Cross, and turn right (COUNTISBURY) along the wide verge. Pass the BRENDON turn, then at the fingerpost cross the road and a stile.

Walk ahead, following yellow waymarks and keeping the wall on your right, to join the short cut at a footpath junction*. Walk on through fields (i.e. turn right if you used the short cut) and around the back of Kipscombe Farm (to the left of the trees). Take the footpath ahead, keeping the field edge on your right.

Cross a tarmac lane and walk ahead for 50m. Fork left where the track divides. Fork left again at the next path division and continue over open moorland to the car park.

To visit the Blue Ball, either retrace your steps to Countisbury or collect your car and drive down to the inn's car park.

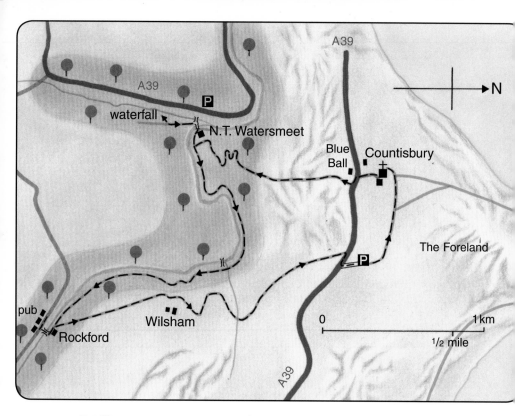

Walk 5 Watersmeet and the Rockford Inn

Distance: 8.1 km (5 miles) Time: 2³/₄ hours
Character: Two steep ascents and one steep descent are amply
rewarded by spectacular views of two deep river gorges and the rocky
coast. This is one of the West Country's most beautiful riverside walks.
It could be linked with Walk 4. On the way are the Rockford Inn, the
Blue Ball and a National Trust tearoom.

Park in the pay-and-display at Watersmeet. Take the gravelled path downhill. Cross a footbridge and divert right up steps, WATERFALL VIEWPOINT. After seeing the waterfall, retrace your steps to the footbridge. Do not return across it, but turn right and cross a second bridge to the National Trust's shop/tearoom/information centre – formerly a shooting and fishing lodge.

The scene is most dramatic after heavy rain, with the river in spate. However, no one would wish for a repeat of the 1952 flood. Over 225 mm (9 inches) had fallen on Exmoor in two days. Powered by

more water than flows down the Thames in three months, the flood swept away houses and cars and killed 34 people.

Leaving the tearoom, turn left upriver, soon signed PUBLIC FOOTPATH ROCKFORD. Continue for some 2.25km along the riverbank. Pass Rockford Lodge, then cross the footbridge about 100m further on. Turn right to visit the Rockford Inn.

Now, retrace your steps to Rockford Lodge and turn right. Walk up through the trees and continue ahead, WILSHAM. At the T-junction ahead, keep left and follow a series of waymarks north, two marked COUNTISBURY. After winding around Wilsham, the path descends to a brook, then climbs steeply to the A39, signed BARNA BARROW.

Turn right up the road for 60m, then left into and through the National Trust car park. Keep the wall on your left and follow the path round to Countisbury church. Walk through the churchyard and down towards the Blue Ball. Turn left up the main road for 60m.

Turn right, WATERSMEET VIA TRILLY RIDGE. Follow the walled path to a field. Continue ahead, WATERSMEET. Keep the wall 50m to your left to find a path downhill through the furze, and through a gate to a footpath junction. Continue ahead, WATERSMEET. The path soon descends very steeply through dense woodland. At a T-junction, turn sharp right and continue downhill to Watersmeet. Retrace your steps across the footbridges to the car park.

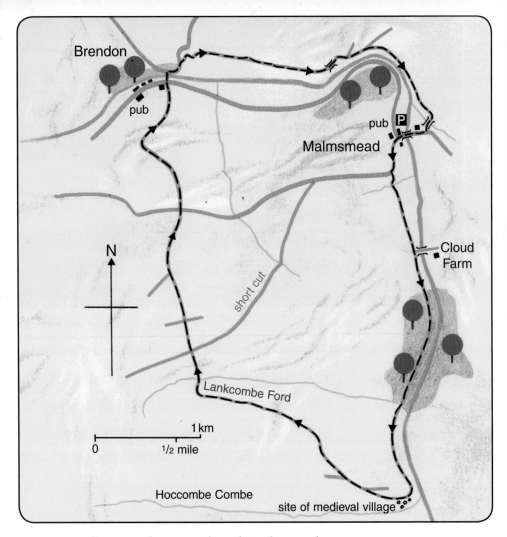

Map labels: Brendon, pub, Malmsmead, pub, P, N, Cloud Farm, short cut, Lankcombe Ford, 1 km, 0, ½ mile, Hoccombe Combe, site of medieval village

Walk 6   Malmsmead and Badgworthy

Distance: 13.5 km (8¹/₂ miles) Time: 4¹/₂ hours
Character: This classic walk has all the vital Exmoor ingredients:
windswept moorland, deep wooded valleys cut by sparkling rivers and
a patchwork of green fields with the restless sea beyond. The route
includes a deserted medieval village, used by R D Blackmore in his
celebrated Exmoor novel 'Lorna Doone' as the stronghold of the
Doones, the dastardly robber band. A relatively easy walk for the
distance, the route has one steep ascent and two steep descents.
Map and compass essential.

Start from Lorna Doone Farm at Malmsmead – the probable origin for Jan Ridd's home in the novel – where refreshments are available at the inn. Take LANE LEADING TO PUBLIC FOOTPATH DOONE VALLEY (or pay 50p and use the riverbank path). After 250m bear left, PUBLIC BRIDLEWAY BADGWORTHY WATER.

At Cloud Farm continue ahead (BRIDLEWAY DOONE VALLEY) following the river for 2.5km. Just beyond the next sign, BRENDON COMMON LARKBARROW, the path curves right. On the left is an abandoned medieval village. Its bracken-covered ruins are typical of local longhouses, with one room for the farmer's family and one for the animals. It has decayed greatly since Blackmore wrote in 1869 – you need imagination to see the Doones in all their wicked splendour.

Return to the track, which rises steadily, curving away from Badgworthy Water. Keep right on the better used fork when the track divides. Several tracks converge on Lankcombe Ford. Keep ahead, bearing north. At the crossways ahead, you could take a short cut by turning right (MALMSMEAD) on a bridleway which cuts north-east across Malmsmead Hill, where you turn right onto Post Lane and follow it to the start. (We have not checked this route recently.)

For the full route continue ahead, BRIDLEWAY BRENDON and enjoy the view. At the next signpost continue ahead, BRIDLEWAY BRENDON,

and again for BRENDON when you reach Cross Gate on a tarred lane. Descend to the village.

(To visit the Staghunters, turn left at Leeford Green, SIMONSBATH BARNSTAPLE. Afterwards, retrace your steps to Leeford Green.)

Turn left LYNMOUTH, cross the bridge and turn right, PORLOCK. Follow the lane to a ladder stile, FOOTPATH COUNTY GATE MALMSMEAD. The path winds uphill, then follows the side of the valley.

Cross a footbridge and turn left, following the curving path uphill. At the top of the rise the path divides. Keep right, on the lower path, go through a gate and take the lower path, MALMSMEAD OARE.

Descend to the river and follow the bankside path round to the second footbridge. Cross and walk up to the tarred lane. Turn right and follow the lane back to Lorna Doone Farm.

Refreshments

This walk offers a very good choice of refreshment stops. The Lorna Doone Inn (photo above) and Cloud Farm Tea Room both offer teas, lunches and cream teas with gardens overlooking Badgworthy Water. At Brendon, the Staghunter's Inn is a traditional country pub thought to date from the 18th century. It has a beer garden next to the East Lyn river.

Walk 7 Exford and the Exe Valley

Distance: 8 km (5 miles) Time: 3 hours
Character: A first class Exmoor route which offers great views and
combines moorland rambling with a beautiful riverside path. Watch
out for deer. The walk follows bridleways and footpaths, with one steep
ascent and one steep descent – with loose stones, so take care.

Start from Exford's signed car park (SS 853384). Walk to the far
end. Continue through a gate with a yellow waymark for 400 m to a
path junction. Turn right, PUBLIC FOOTPATH COURT FARM. Turn left
at Court Farm, BRIDLEWAY TO ROOM HILL. Follow the track around
the farm. When the lane bends sharp right, bear left through a gate,
BRIDLEWAY ROOM HILL.

Continue steeply uphill. Extensive views open out as the path
leaves Court Copse. At the signed junction turn right (PUBLIC
BRIDLEWAY ROOM HILL) through a characteristic Exmoor beech
hedgebank. Continue on level ground. Keep left when the track forks
(NETHERCOTE) around the head of a deep combe. Keep left again after
450 m, WINSFORD.

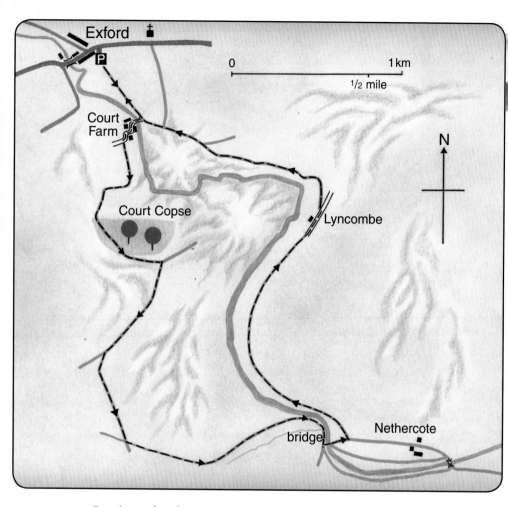

Continue ahead over grass, past an abandoned harrow and on to a blue marker post. Bear left, following the bridleway steeply downhill and parallel to a gully. Reaching the river, turn right for 50 m.

Cross the bridge. Continue uphill (BRIDLEWAY LYNCOMBE) for 150 m. Turn sharp left, BRIDLEWAY LYNCOMBE. Just beyond Lyncombe, turn left over a stile, FOOTPATH TO EXFORD. Continue to a ford. Don't cross the river. Turn right over a stile and follow the footpath along the east bank of the river. Continue on the footpath as it diverges away from the river and climbs. Continue to Court Farm, ignoring side turnings. Turn right and retrace your steps to the car park. For refreshments, continue into Exford.

Refreshments

Opposite the car park is the Crown Hotel which has an interesting collection of local photographs and sporting prints. Turn left towards the river for Exford Bridge Tea Rooms. Beyond is the Exmoor White Horse.

The White Horse is said to date from the 16th century. Country sports are extensively represented, with a magnificent stag's head in the hall and a collection of photos in the large bar, plus trophies of the chase. The dining room has many landscape colour photographs, mainly local scenes, by the landlord.

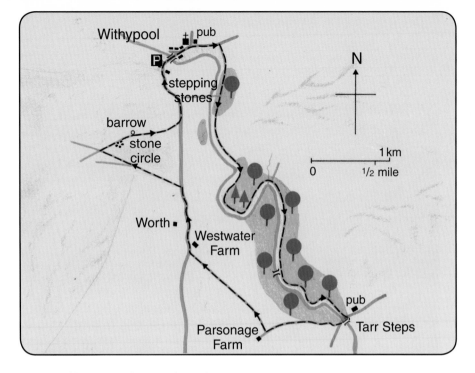

Walk 8   Withypool and Tarr Steps

Distance: 13.4km (8¹/₄ miles) Time: 4¹/₄ hours
Character: This superb Exmoor walk combines a beautiful riverbank path with open moorland, field paths and quiet lanes. As well as Tarr Steps, one of the moor's most fascinating historic structures, there is a prehistoric stone circle and also a barrow on Withypool Hill. At 398m, the hill offers wonderful panoramic views. Three steep ascents. Some parts can be very muddy after rain. Do not attempt this walk if the river is in spate. Take a compass.

Turn left out of the free car park in Withypool (SS 845354). Cross the bridge, built in traditional fashion in 1866. Continue past the post office stores and the church with its curiously squat tower. Walk on past the Royal Oak and follow the lane uphill. Cross a stile on the right, TARR STEPS. Simply follow the path parallel to the River Barle for the next 5.7km, ignoring side turnings, to Tarr Steps.

Tarr Steps is immediately impressive. This 36m long clapper bridge is built of 17 flat slabs of stone, each weighing two tonnes and over two metres long. Most authorities now agree that the present structure

is medieval. To the left of Tarr Steps is Tarr Farm, now an inn and restaurant offering refreshments all year.

Cross Tarr Steps and fork right almost immediately, PUBLIC BRIDLEWAY PARSONAGE FARM WESTWATER FARM. Follow the blue waymarks and stony track steeply uphill, swinging right then turning left before a field gate. Continue uphill then gently down towards Parsonage Farm.

Turn right (WITHYPOOL HILL) at the gate leading to Parsonage Farm. Follow the track through a series of fields and gates with blue waymarks. Walk ahead, WITHYPOOL, at the next signpost.

Arriving at a lane, turn right, WITHYPOOL VIA ROAD. Follow the lane past Westwater Farm and uphill to a cattle grid. Turn left, BRIDLEWAY WITHYPOOL HILL. Follow the track, keeping the hedge on your left until it ends. Keep right when the bridleway forks.

After 550 m a fainter track crosses the bridleway at an angle. Turn sharp right and follow it uphill. Aim for the mound on the summit and follow the rough path past a stone circle. If you have a GPS, the circle is at SS 8384 3432. It can easily be missed as the stones are very low and several are missing or buried. Enjoy the views from the barrow on the summit, then follow the rough path eastward. Turn left onto a lane and follow it downhill to the start.

Withypool has both a pub (see page 31) and a tea room.

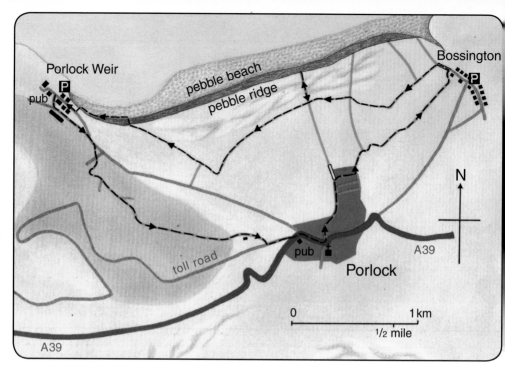

Walk 9   Bossington and Porlock

Distance: 10km (6¹/₄ miles) Time: 3 hours
Character: Although mainly level, this walk offers great views of
Porlock Bay and the surrounding hills. Since floods broke through the
bay's pebble ridge in 1996, it is no longer possible to walk its entire
length but much of it can be explored from the marsh path described
here. Note that this path should be avoided during high tides and after
heavy rain. There are three attractive villages on the way, all with one
or more eateries – including two Ship Inns (see page 32).

Park in the National Trust car park at Bossington. Turn right out of
the car park, COAST PATH. Keep right at Myrtle Cottage. Follow the
lane to a path junction and continue ahead, COAST PATH PORLOCK
WEIR. Turn left 100m ahead, COAST PATH PORLOCK WEIR VIA MARSH.
Follow the coast path with its yellow waymarks and/or acorn signs.

The pebble ridge was formed 8000 years ago. It was breached in
1996; subsequent storms moved the beach 20-30m inland, cutting a
canyon through the marsh clay and turning freshwater marsh into
tidal marsh, often visited by shelducks, oystercatchers, gulls and curlews.

24

Unless the tide is high, divert right (BEACH) to view the pebble ridge from its crest, then retrace your steps to the fingerpost and turn right for PORLOCK WEIR. On the way are a number of skeletons of trees killed by the invading salt.

Follow COAST PATH PORLOCK WEIR VIA MARSH at the next junction (or divert inland, PORLOCK, if the marsh is flooded). The path briefly crosses onto the beach. Then join the road and continue to Porlock Weir with its pretty harbour.

Facing the Ship Inn, take the lane uphill past the telephone booth. Continue ahead at the junction and past cottages to a T-junction.

Turn right, and after just 75m right again onto an unsigned but obvious footpath. Cross a lane and follow the well-beaten path and various PORLOCK signs through the woods to join another lane, which leads down to a second Ship Inn.

Continue past the Ship and follow Porlock's main street, past the church. Take the next turning left, SPARKHAYES LANE. Continue ahead past side-streets and a no-through-road sign. Turn next right up steps. Continue along a street. At the far end turn left, BOSSINGTON.

Keep right at the path junction, BOSSINGTON. Turn right at the next path junction. Go through a kissing gate and turn left. Continue to a lane and turn right, COAST PATH BOSSINGTON. Retrace your steps to the car park. There's a tearoom (photo on page 1) opposite.

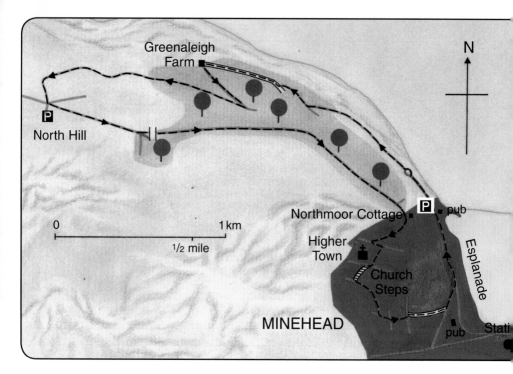

Walk 10   Minehead and North Hill

Distance: 7.8km (4³/₄ miles)   Time: 2¹/₂ hours
Character: A long climb through woodland from Minehead's attractive
harbour to North Hill (247m), with a couple of steep sections, is
rewarded with superb views across to Wales, and south over Exmoor.
The latter part of the walk is gently downhill through woodland
to Minehead's historic Higher Town, which has a splendid church
and many thatched cottages. There are numerous pubs and cafés in
Minehead.

Park towards the western end of the Esplanade or in the Quay Road
West car park. The walk starts at the Ship Aground, beside the harbour. Head away from the town. The road soon ends and there is a
tarmac path parallel to the beach. Later it becomes an earthen path
which heads inexorably uphill. Keep right at all junctions, COAST
PATH, then join a tarmac track. Continue ahead. There are good views
of Greenaleigh Point below on your right.

　　Just before you reach Greenaleigh Farm, turn left up steps, COAST
PATH PORLOCK. This climbs steadily at a diagonal to the hillside, up to

a bench. Turn sharp right (COAST PATH) and continue uphill, emerging onto furze- and bracken-clad cliffs.

When the path doglegs, follow it sharp left, climbing steeply to a footpath junction. Take a rest on the bench to enjoy the views and then turn left on BRIDLEWAY MINEHEAD.

After 600 m the path divides into three. Keep left and walk ahead MINEHEAD. Descend gently through woodland along the broad path, ignoring side turnings.

Continue ahead onto the tarmac, past Northmoor Cottage and downhill to a T junction. Turn left and continue downhill.

Take the next right turn, CHURCH ROAD, and walk down to St Michael's, which displays an illuminated missal dating from 1320, as well as having a carved screen, a clock jack, and much else of interest and beauty.

Turn right at the church gate. Turn left after 25 m, down CHURCH STEPS. Walk down past the thatched cottages. Turn left into CHURCH STREET, then left into MIDDLE STREET. Keep right, then turn left into CLANVILLE STREET. At the bottom of this street follow the footpath ahead down to the Esplanade. Turn left (or right for the Hobby Horse, see page 32) and into Quay Town with its old buildings.

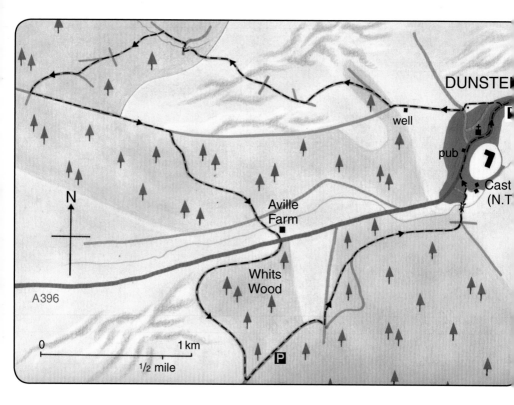

Walk 11 Dunster

Distance: 10km (6¼ miles) Time: 4 hours
Character: A seriously demanding exploration of the hills and woods
near Dunster. Attention needed to directions. At the end of the walk,
you may wish to explore the town, where there are numerous eateries.

Park in the car park at the north end of Dunster (SS993439). Walk towards the town, then, 50m beyond the Visitor Centre, turn right into THE BALL. When the lane turns left, continue ahead (PRIVATE DRIVE – FOOTPATH ACCESS). At the top of the tarmac drive continue ahead on a footpath across a field to the medieval butter cross.

Turn left down ST GEORGE'S STREET. After 80m, turn right into BRIDLEWAY GRABBIST HILL. Just beyond St Leonard's Well, the path divides at a deer gate. Fork right, ELLICOMBE. After 150m, bear left (BRIDLEWAY) and head uphill through a gate. Turn right at the next path junction, MINEHEAD. Keep left when the path divides, and continue ahead (ALCOMBE) and again, YOUTH HOSTEL.

28

At a tarred lane, turn right, then after 50 m left, TIMBERSCOMBE. The path turns left after 200 m (WOOTON COMMON), crosses the stream and climbs steeply. Keep left at the fork. Bear right near the summit (WOOTON COMMON) and continue to a path junction. Turn left for just 10 m to a path crossing.

Turn left, DUNSTER. This path offers superb views of the coast and eventually returns to the deer gate near St Leonard's Well. You may wish to shorten the walk in this way. If not, continue on the path for 1 km, then turn right, BRIDLEWAY AVILLE FARM.

When the bridleway divides, turn right and steeply downhill at the next blue waymark. Cross the tarred lane. Continue ahead, over the footbridge to the road. Cross with care. Walk ahead.

Follow the path uphill to a gate, then around the edge of Whits Wood. When the path divides, keep ahead. Keep right at the next division. Turn right again at the next division and walk on to a three-way marker post. This time, don't take the Timberscombe option but turn left (BRIDLEWAY) and continue to a tarred lane.

Turn left and follow the lane downhill past Nutcombe Bottom car park. Do not take the lane to Broadwood Farm. Walk on for 50 m. Bear

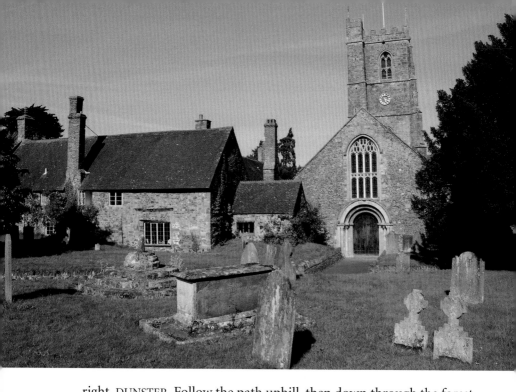

right, DUNSTER. Follow the path uphill, then down through the forest.

Keep ahead (DUNSTER) at the next junction and cross medieval Gallox Bridge. Reaching the entrance to a car park, continue ahead up the footpath to a T-junction. Turn left (unless you wish to visit the mill or its tearooms) and follow the mill leat up to West Street.

Turn right, and you will see the Stag's Head on your left. Continue to the 1499 Priory church and round to the main street, past the Yarn Market (1609) and the medieval Luttrell Arms, to the car park.

The Stag's Head

This is a listed medieval building with many interesting features. It began as an open hall-house, the smoke from the open fires simply percolating upwards and out through the roof. In the guest rooms, jointed cruck beams and timber framing are exposed. One room has a fresco and is thought to have a hidden cavity or 'priest-hole' behind. Downstairs there are more exposed beams and masonry. Log fires occupy two stone hearths.

The Stag's Head is a friendly, family-run inn open all year, offering food at lunchtimes and evenings.

Pubs with stories

The Royal Oak, Withypool is a sporting inn of a traditional character. Trophies of the chase, sporting prints, hunting and wildlife photographs decorate both bars, which have open fires and comfortable seats and tables. The building is thought to be over 300 years old and retains its old fireplaces and exposed ceiling beams..

Perhaps drawn by its quiet and isolated position, several distinguished and unexpected people have been associated with the Royal Oak. R D Blackmore wrote part of *Lorna Doone* in the bar, the artist Alfred Munnings had a studio in the loft, and General Eisenhower planned parts of the D-Day landings here.

From 1927-35, Gwladys and Maxwell Knight owned the inn. Knight was a bit different from the average innkeeper. Later known to millions as a TV and radio naturalist, he also had a secret career with MI5, which he joined in 1925. Knight became a spy-master at the heart of events and played a key counter-espionage role before and during the Second World War, infiltrating both the Communist Party and Oswald Mosley's British Union of Fascists.

One of Knight's agents was Ian Fleming, who modelled the character M in his James Bond stories on his boss, whose real life story far outshines Fleming's fiction. Ask at the bar to see Knight's portrait.

The Ship Inn, Porlock is said to date from 1290, so it is one of England's oldest inns, with a thatched roof, exposed beams, gothic window, huge open fireplaces and a 'lateral' chimneystack (placed in the side wall rather than an end wall). 'Southey's Corner' is located in this chimneystack, honouring Poet Laureate Robert Southey who at the Ship wrote a sonnet celebrating Porlock in 1798.

Licencees of the Ship have been traced back to 1744, when most travellers arrived on foot or horseback or by boat; wheeled transport was virtually unknown on Exmoor. With the coming of turnpike roads and stagecoaches, stabling was developed at the Ship, which provided extra horses to drag coaches up notorious Porlock Hill.

The Ship Inn, Porlock Weir (photo above) is known as 'The Bottom Ship', to distinguish it from 'the Top Ship' in Porlock. It is built of beach stone with lime mortar, has exposed beams and lateral chimneystacks.

The Hobby Horse Inn, Minehead was originally part of the Metropole Hotel, and partakes in its Victorian opulence. It gets its name from Minehead's May Day Hobby horse celebrations. Ask to see the dining room with its impressive plaster ceiling, and the remarkable Victorian baroque ballroom.